BELIEVE
IN
YOUR
INNER
VOICE

ROSEMARY NAPOLITAN

BALBOA.PRESS
A DIVISION OF HAY HOUSE

Balboa Press books may be ordered through booksellers or by contacting:

Balboa Press
A Division of Hay House
1663 Liberty Drive
Bloomington, IN 47403
www.balboapress.com
1 (877) 407-4847

Because of the dynamic nature of the Internet, any web addresses or links contained in this book may have changed since publication and may no longer be valid. The views expressed in this work are solely those of the author and do not necessarily reflect the views of the publisher, and the publisher hereby disclaims any responsibility for them.

The author of this book does not dispense medical advice or prescribe the use of any technique as a form of treatment for physical, emotional, or medical problems without the advice of a physician, either directly or indirectly. The intent of the author is only to offer information of a general nature to help you in your quest for emotional and spiritual well-being. In the event you use any of the information in this book for yourself, which is your constitutional right, the author and the publisher assume no responsibility for your actions.

Any people depicted in stock imagery provided by Getty Images are models, and such images are being used for illustrative purposes only.
Certain stock imagery © Getty Images.

Print information available on the last page.

ISBN: 978-1-9822-4511-5 (sc)
ISBN: 978-1-9822-4510-8 (e)

Library of Congress Control Number: 2020905180

Balboa Press rev. date: 03/19/2020

Contents

Year 1953

Before I was born, my pregnant mom, in her seventh month, fell down the stairs and injured one leg severely to the point of almost losing it. She held onto me as she fell down the stairs and in the ambulance on the way to the hospital, she prayed to God to keep me safe and she would name me Mary (after the Blessed Virgin Mary) and my dad wanted to name me Rose after his sister, Rose. Amazingly, I was born healthy and my mom's leg healed by the grace of God, good medical care and the love of her family. I lost a little weight while in the long stay at the hospital, but I made up for it as soon as I went home.

From that point on, my life has been lived by my faith in God and his divine plan. I have experienced miracles and I can feel when my life is going to take a turn in direction. I can also feel the spiritual support and I have seen and connected spiritually with family, friends and pets that have gone to Heaven. I am not trying to convince you of anything. I am simply sharing my experiences with you so you may experience the comfort, peace and support that I feel in my life.

After my tumultuous experience at birth, I wanted to be very close to my mom. I have many memories of helping her bake, wash clothes, can food and decorate the house for the holidays. My favorite memory was when I was in grade school and she and

1

I walked to the Department Store and tried on lady's hats of all shapes and sizes and we laughed so hard, we almost wet our pants. My mom and I both loved Christmas as our favorite holiday. She also taught me how to embroider and to crochet when I was a young girl. She liked to sew and I later learned to sew in junior high school. From that point on, we crafted together to the point of attending craft shows to sell our creations and then converting our house to a craft boutique right before the holidays, inviting the general public in to shop. **I felt this was my first time that I knew I was living my life purpose because I was very happy, it felt natural and we were successful financially even though our real joy was seeing others enjoy our creations.**

Year 1966

In junior high and high school, I made some lifelong friends and I wanted to be a Teacher as a career. At the beginning of 7th grade, my family moved us to California. I went to the first day of school not knowing anyone. I received my schedule of classes and was standing there alone when a girl with VERY tight perm in her hair asked me what classes I had. We compared our papers and the schedules were EXACTLY the SAME. She said her name and she was new to California and I said, me, too. Little did we know we would be BEST Friends/Soul Mates for LIFE. She has been more like a sister to me and is the only person who "gets" me completely. She is my soul sister!

Year 1973

In 1972 I graduated from high school. A few times I went on outings with my older sister and her husband. They had a beautiful Irish Setter dog and they entered him in dog shows. A day or so before the Show, my sister called me and said her husband and she had an opportunity to go snow skiing instead. She told me she was torn because she really wanted to go to the dog show and asked me what she should do. **I thought a few moments and I felt strongly that she should go to the dog show and I told her so. Well she decided to go skiing for the very first time.** She ended up suffering in a horrific accident and broke both of her legs and ankles and continues to have ankle surgeries. **I felt I had a premonition and felt so bad for her.**

In high school I had a calling that I was to be a nun. I was surprised but I thought about it a while and then the feeling faded and I attended Junior College. When I graduated from Junior College, I took a year off and helped my mom around the house. I thought I would go to a 4-year college to get my teaching degree. But that summer, my life took a turn.

Year 1975

My dad told me to get a summer job or he was going to get me into HP as a summer hire. My dad and I were always close, but I did not want to work for HP as my father worked there and I felt he would be checking on me all the time. I was unsuccessful getting a job on my own, so I worked at HP. I figured it would just be for the summer, but after working 3 weeks, the supervisor told me I was doing an excellent job and she wanted to hire me on permanently. **Once again, this felt surprisingly RIGHT for me and as it turned out, there were very few teacher job openings at that time.** I thought I would just work a little until I could discover another direction and return to college. Well, that job at HP turned into many jobs and two career re-directions over the next 32 years. I was promoted many times and achieved much success, recognition, and reward. **I began to question God as to why I was making so much money. I was a single woman. What was his plan for me?**

During these years, I began to experience spiritual encounters with family, pets and friends that have gone to heaven. My grandmother on my dad's side and I were very close as I take after her in many ways and the morning she died, her spirit stood at the foot of my bed and I awoke to a cold feeling and her calling my name. I saw her smiling and then she was gone. Within the hour, my dad called me and told me she had died. My grandmother and her mother were VERY SPIRITUAL and GIFTED and practiced healing other people. I feel very close to them and I will share my other spiritual experiences with you.

I became very good friends with an elderly mother of a friend of mine who was German like my mom. I would visit her and we would talk for hours. She was not the first elderly woman I spent time with. This started early in my childhood with an elderly woman who lived across the street from us when I was 5 or 6 and of course I loved to spend time with both of my grandmothers. Well, one night I was sleeping and awoke to a very cold room again, and this time it was her spirit standing at the side of my bed, smiling and saying she was fine. Later that morning, my friend told me she had passed away early that morning. I think I realized I was comfortable and fascinated with elderly women for some specific reason.

Year 1977

During the summer, my parents and two of my sisters and I went by motorhome across the country to visit family in Pennsylvania. We were somewhere in Nebraska where you can see nothing for miles and all of a sudden, the motorhome started sputtering like the engine was going to die. I was riding up front with my dad and my mom and sisters were in the back of the motorhome. I could see my dad was VERY worried by looking at his face, so I began to pray to God for help. I prayed that he would get us to the next town safely so we could get it fixed instead of being stranded out in the middle of nowhere. I kept praying and the engine was beginning to die so my dad pulled off the road that dipped down like a ravine so you could not clearly see us from the road now and the engine died. No cars saw us pulling off because we were the only ones on the desolate highway. I looked to the right and only seeing mountains **very far away,** I kept praying.

My dad told me to go to the back of the motorhome so he could lift the cover to look at the motor. When I sat down, I looked to the right and I was shocked to see a short stocky man with a straw hat on with his back to us and his hands crossed behind him. I swear he looked just like my dad's father who had passed away some time before. I told my dad; maybe that guy over there can help you. He said, "What guy?" No one else could see him. I thought that was odd. Then I looked again and he was gone. Right after that, I looked out the back window and I saw what looked like an older man and woman and a younger man and woman with a dog walking toward our motorhome. They did not have any car and if they did it would have been behind us. The women were wearing pedal pusher pants that were not popular at that time and the younger woman had old fashioned curlers in her hair. I yelled to my dad that some people were coming. This time every one of us could see them. They came alongside the motorhome and my dad opens the side door to talk to them. They asked if they could help. My dad said he was having trouble with the transmission. One of the men looked at the transmission, put his hand on it, and said, "Why don't you try to start it now? ".

Well, it started right up and the guy said you should be good to go now. My dad thanked them and offered to give them something. They said "No thank you, we help people all the time out here." So, my dad closed the door and they walked towards the rear of the motorhome. My dad called to me so I turned my head for a second or 2 and then quickly looked back to see where they were going and they vanished completely as quickly as they appeared. The motorhome made it to the nearest town where the transmission failed again and we were there 2 days until the parts arrived and it was fixed. **Did God answer my prayers? Absolutely YES!**

Year 1980's

At this time, I began to understand why I did not become a nun. My next walk in life was to care for my parents in their elder years. As I grew up and began working, I was able to buy a house with them at first, then they wanted to move closer to my brothers and sisters and my dad wanted to retire. I found two homes a block apart and purchased them with the profit from our home we sold. My father could now retire early. I continued to support and care for my parents.

Year 1994

During these years, my career kept accelerating with responsibility and salary and I was able to support my parents and myself. I dated a few men, but none of them seemed to be THE man for me. **So, I thought maybe this is my walk- in- life and continued on.** Then one weekend, a niece came to spend the weekend with me. My allergies had been bothering me and it felt like maybe I was getting a cold settling in my throat. We were relaxing when my niece fell asleep on the sofa and I was feeling worse sitting in my lounger. I started to doze and a voice woke me and told me to go to the hospital. Now this would never have been MY idea! I rarely went to the doctor. The feeling was so strong that I felt someone was pushing me. So, I woke my niece and when I asked her to drive me to the hospital, I scared her awake and she jumped up. I told her we'll just go get some antibiotics so we can have a good weekend visit. By the time we got to the hospital, I felt amazingly well and told her I did not want to sound like a hypochondriac but she said let's go get checked since we were there. Well they took me back to a room and did an EKG and within seconds, my room was filled with nurses and doctors putting needles and IV's in me and asking me what my pain level was at least 10 times and I was in NO pain. They did not believe me and told me I was having a heart attack. I thought they must be mistaken, but then I was worried as they **ran** with me on the gurney to the Intensive care unit. As soon as I got there, they asked me if my heart stopped, did I want to be resuscitated. I was 40 years old! I said, "Hell YES!" Then I would not close my eyes or sleep all night because I thought I was going to die! During the week I was in the hospital, they injected die in my arteries and said one large artery was 100% blocked. The reason I did not die is that on my way to the hospital, my blood that was blocked had rerouted through some smaller arteries which is a rare occurrence so I would not need surgery. **They said they usually only find this to happen with athletes due to their body conditioning and strength. WOW! I realized my walk-in life was not over and I needed to take better care of myself.**

I exercised regularly and radically changed my diet. I began taking medicine that would be a lifelong need. When I went in for a treadmill test, months later, the test showed that my blockage was cleared! **One could argue this was all due to the changes and medicine, but I believe I know I had help from God! I have not had ANY further heart trouble and it has been 25 years since that day.**

Year 1995

After my heart attack. I realized I needed to take more vacations or time off from work to relieve stress. A friend of mine referred me to a timeshare in Southern California in Palm Desert close to Palm Springs. I checked it out with another friend one weekend and I bought into the timeshare resort. I had one week each year reserved to use one of the units, fully furnished with cooking and laundry and access to golf and all amenities at the resort. It had sleeping accommodations for eight people. So, I could take several friends with me to have a good time. I decided this would push me to go on vacation at least once a year and get away from the stress. For the first year, my closest niece wanted to go and all of my friends could not get away. So, my niece drove her car and she and I went. There were some outlets close by so we drove there and had fun shopping. To go back to the resort, we had to use an underpass of the freeway and we were in the left- hand turn lane at a red light. At a right angle from us was a very long truck and trailer or a motorhome making a left-hand turn in front of us. I could see he had turned too sharp and he was going to hit us and we could not move due to traffic behind us. I started yelling, "he is going to hit us, he is going to hit us!" My niece was frozen and then all of a sudden, my niece's vehicle lifted in the air, moved us to the right and put us down again just in time so the truck and trailer did not hit us! My niece looked at me and I looked at her in shock**! EITHER GOD OR OUR GUARDIAN ANGELS LIFTED OUR VEHICLE AND SAVED US FROM DANGER!!**

Year 1997-98

I could not have imagined my strong parents would need me so much in their retirement years. The next several years would be the hardest in my life!

Year 1999

At this time, I also had 2 Cocker Spaniel dogs that my mom and I loved dearly. Molly was my first Cocker and I bought her when she was 6 weeks old and she was my baby. As she aged she had many health problems and I had to make the hardest decision to put her to sleep. That day, my heart broke. I was crying so hard when I came home and decided to try to get my mind occupied on something else so I went outside to water some bushes in my yard. My Molly knew I did not like her kissing me on my mouth so she would always kiss me in my ear. Well, when I went outside toward the bushes, all of a sudden in my side vision, I saw something flying fast toward me and smacking me in my right ear. I shook my head and thought it was a bee. But then I looked up and saw it was a beautiful golden butterfly with colors I have never seen in a butterfly and it was circling my head. To this day, I do not know why I said the next dialogue out loud, "Molly, is that you? It kept circling and I walked over to the bushes and started watering a bush. The butterfly rested on the curb in front of the bush and didn't seem to mind the hose spray. I told her I loved her and I missed her. As I moved left to the next bush and to 4 or 5 more bushes, each time, the butterfly moved down to each bush and rested on the curb or on the bush in front of me. I then backed up and said, "Molly, I will be ok. You can go now in peace." The butterfly then flew up above my head, circled two times and flew away. That night when I was asleep, I awoke suddenly and beside my bed on the floor was Molly sitting there. I said, "Molly, I love you". She was very happy and said back in a weird tone, "I love you more." Then she was gone.

Year 2001

Months later, I kept getting this feeling that I was going to be asked to do something very important. Then I got this feeling that I had to redecorate one of my upstairs spare bedrooms in a Victorian female décor. I did not know why but I needed to do it quickly so I did. Within a month or so, a niece called me and unexpectedly on her part and mine, said she needed to move. She moved into my newly decorated room, which she helped me to decorate in Victorian décor (that she ALSO likes), and stayed with me for 7 or 8 months. After she left, another family member in need came to live with me for a few months, then another niece needed to find a temporary place and she and her son lived in that room for about a year and lastly a nephew needed a place to stay for a short time and he lived there, too. **My house was like a revolving door for a long while for those in need.**

Then, my mom was diagnosed with Alzheimer's. When my mom got Alzheimer's, this was my most trying time of my life. Everything previous in my life prepared me for this responsibility/ blessing and I felt it coming. **This was the important responsibility I was expecting to have.** And I cared for my mom for all but the last two years of her life. I was blessed with reading materials and support groups and the help of family, but most of all, I was supported by God every day. **The question I kept asking about**

was why I was making so much money was answered; so, I could retire early and to take care of myself and my mother. So, I retired and I was completely at peace with that major turn in my life because I knew it was my destiny.

Year 2004

One day I woke up and planned to go to my niece's house. I was in a light mood and got in the car anxious to see her. Her mom is my best friend and soulmate I told you about previously. My friend's parents unofficially adopted me as their third daughter as I spent much time at their house and they became part of our family later. My friend had three children, two daughters and one son. I am driving down the freeway to one of her daughter's house and I feel someone is in my backseat. It is my friend's deceased mom and with no control of my mouth, I say her name out loud, "Are you in my backseat?" She said yes. I said, "I miss you. How are you?" I told her I was going to her granddaughter's house. She said she was always proud of her granddaughter. I asked why she was visiting me. She said she is worried about her grandkids. I said, "Don't worry. I will look after them ". She said, "I'm particularly worried about one of them." I knew who she was worried about. I said, "Ok, I will look after them." I told her not to worry. She said thank you and she was gone. Needless to say, I kept driving, but could not get over the feeling of talking to someone from heaven. My mouth spoke words but I guess my soul was communicating. So, I arrived at my niece's home and told her what happened. She is close enough to me to know I have these experiences, but was puzzled about her grandmother's worry too. Well, only a few days later, I received a call from her mom that one of her children had a serious crisis. That's why my friend's mom came to me. **Oh my! Our loved ones DO look after us from heaven!**

Years 2007-2012

As my mom progressed into later stages of Alzheimer's, I was able to hire some caregivers to come into my house and stay with her when I needed to go out or just to get some respite time. **I began to get another strong feeling that I was going to be doing something with children but the children were not mine. It became clear when my mom finally moved to my sister's location in South Carolina.** Now alone, I rented my mom's room to a mother and daughter who became friends with me. Later my dad and his second wife needed a place to stay so they moved into my house, too. I looked on Craig's List and the first job I applied for was very close to my house. I did not think I would hear anything because it takes applying for many jobs most times to get one to respond, but in a few days, they called and wanted to interview me! I went to the interview but they were looking for someone who could speak fluent Spanish. I knew a little, but was not fluent. Weeks went by so I applied for another job at an Insurance Company. Lo and behold, they called, too, and wanted to interview me. I was very surprised! The day I was supposed to go to the interview, they called me and said the guy who was to interview me was sick and would have to reschedule with me. Within an hour after that call, the first company called me again and offered me a different job! **You will not be surprised when I tell you the name of the company was Child Development Center! I guess this was the answer to my feeling about doing something with children!**

Year 2014

My mom lived to be 88 years old and in her final days in a rest home near my sister. One night I was lying in bed and awake and I noticed that my hands were intertwined and my thumbs twirling. I thought this was weird and then I realized why as I sensed my Mother's Dad in my room and he said to me," We are all here waiting for her and it will not be long now." My grandfather was known for intertwining his hands like that and twirling his thumbs. That very day, I and my siblings and my dad had called her and with the phone held up to her ear, we all told her we loved her and we were ok so she could go in peace.

The next morning, my sisters experienced the bright light in my mother's room and my mom saying, "They are all here and named all of her brothers and sisters and her mom and dad who had already gone to heaven" with a big smile in her voice. They saw a bright light above and our mom went to heaven peacefully.

I stayed at Child Development for two years and quit shortly after my mom died because I felt my job was done there. A lifelong friend of mine unexpectedly called me the very next day at 5am **not knowing** I had quit my job and said that she had this very strong feeling that she needed to call me and ask me to work for her as she had an unexpected opening. **She told me the feeling was very strong to call me so early.** I told her she would not believe it, but I just quit my job the day before. She bypassed all protocol to bring me on board immediately and kept saying the job was mine even if it was just temporary till I found something else. This friend has been my mentor, my boss several times at HP and my friend for 32 years!

Three months later, **once again, I had this feeling that my life was going to change again.** I made less money at my friend's job and with a house full of people, expenses were going up and the renters did not have the ability to pay more rent. **I always planned to sell my house later in life, but the feeling to sell now was getting very strong.** I had a dream that I sold my house but I did not dream where I had moved. I started to think where I wanted to live and called one of my brothers, who lived close to a timeshare I used to own in Southern California because I liked the area. **My house sold literally with "ONE" Open House for the price I wanted (against a much lower price the real estate agent wanted me to start with) and within 1 month, I moved out, bought another house two blocks from my brother after looking at it once and immediately knowing it was my next house.** My dad and his second wife separated and he and my dog, Katie moved with me.

My dad stayed with me about nine months and then reunited with his second wife when he woke up one day and said God told him that his wife needed him and he needed to go NOW! That week, I drove him 7 hours to her apartment and 2 weeks later she was diagnosed with a terminal illness.

Year 2015

We have all grieved my birth mom in our own way. It is a year and a half now that she has gone to heaven. This past Mother's Day, I was in my office and thinking about her. All of a sudden, I felt like she was standing right behind me. I turned around and my dog had her head cocked sideways and looking above me as if she was looking at my mom. My dog, Katie, was mesmerized for a long moment before I could get her attention. My dog so loved my mom and spent many years with her, and my mom loved animals! She even fed the wild squirrels and birds daily. I know she is watching over us. Sometimes, I feel her in church as if she is sitting next to me.

Well, here I am again living just with my dog, Katie, in my new residence. **And yes, I am feeling a change coming again. I am not sure how big it is or when it will happen, but I am getting the message to be patient.**

Now it is the 4th of July and I am at my brother's house for a barbecue. For the past several days, a sibling from the Bay Area had been trying to help my dad and was getting no cooperation from anyone. My dad was very distraught and unable to pay the in-home care for his ill wife. I was asked by my sibling to come to the Bay Area and help with their situation as I was very experienced with Social Security, Med-i-Cal, and in-home caregivers with helping my mom. I knew God was asking me to help my dad. I took my dad to Social Security to see if they could get Med-i-Cal. When we arrived, there were probably 100 people there and I figured we would have a long wait. We took a number and took a seat. After 10-15 minutes, they called our name! I looked at my dad and said. "Wow, what about all of the other people here waiting longer than us? The other people looked at us as if asking, "Why do you get preference over us?" My dad and I approached the advisor and within 15-20 minutes of explaining our situation, the man told us that they would qualify for help, but we had to go to a mandatory meeting the following week as a formality and in the meantime, I could start looking to hire an in-home care provider. My dad and I were shocked! The man told us to wait and he would give us the paper with the appointment information. In 5 minutes or so, a man ran over to my dad and handed him the paper. When we got in the car, I had to tell my dad that this was a remarkable experience as all of my experiences with my mom and Social Security involved long waits and lots of paperwork to be completed. Then my dad wanted to go to a funeral home to plan for his second wife's burial ceremony. He and his wife bought their cemetery plot a few years earlier. My dad gave me a list of funeral homes that work with the cemetery. I looked at the list and had no clue how to pick one, but I did and we drove there. Once there, we were the sole customer and had the most informal meeting with the owner's son who treated us like family and gave my dad an estimate that was **very** reasonable. My dad was very relieved. He said he felt like he had known this guy for years! Again, we got in the car and I turned to my dad and said, "I feel God with us today, guiding us, and clearing our path so everything falls into place." My dad agreed with me. I thought my job was done and I could now go home. No, my dad needed me further as I discovered the next day.

The next day, my dad called very distraught and wanted me to come right over. He felt helpless because his wife's condition would not improve. As her children were caring for her, my dad decided to come back to my home and live his remaining years with me. I told my dad that we should seek his attorney's advice and we did. His attorney advised that my dad file for a divorce to protect the rest of my dad's assets and to move away from the stress. **I took my dad to live with me once again. Needless to say, I answered God's call and my sister's request, and I helped my dad so he could live in peace.**

While my dad was living with Fran, I made some new friends from our church and one woman in particular seemed to have so much in common with me. There are too many things to mention that we share in our life journey, but little did I know that I spiritually would experience the following to get her to open up and get even closer to me. Knowing that her husband died a few years earlier, she told me one day that tomorrow would have been their 30th wedding anniversary. I knew she was sad and I wanted to give her something to cheer her up. With my love for flowers, I thought I would bring her some as I planned to go to her house that day regarding church matters. I woke up that day refreshed and the first thing on my mind was to stop and pick up some flowers. I felt a sense of urgency to get to the store. I thought I was just excited because I always like to give someone flowers and to see their face light up. I got to the store and went directly to the flower section and my eyes zeroed in on this spectacular bouquet of red roses. It must have been 1-2 dozen. I thought to myself how beautiful they were as I love red roses and then I said to myself, "She will think I am weird bringing her red roses, especially so many of them as I hardly know her!!" I looked around and found another bouquet of mixed flowers that also had 3 red roses. I said to myself, "Perfect". I paid for them and walked to my car and felt as if someone was pushing me to hurry and get to my friend's house. As I approached my car, I could not help but notice a tree in the parking lot that was right next to my car. It was completely loaded with birds, (at least 50) and they were chirping so loud as if they were talking or singing to me. I said, "Good morning" before I realized I even said it and they sang some more. I happened to look around the parking lot at all of the other trees and there were NO birds in any of the other trees. OK, now I am beginning to feel a spirit is with me. They are anxious that I get to my friend's house. I get into the car and I find myself saying OUTLOUD, "Ok, I am going there now." I can feel the spirit in the car with me and I do not know who it is. I get to my friend's house and I bring the flowers to her door. She opens the door and there's the big smile I expect. I tell her Happy Anniversary and she is so appreciative. At that moment, I figured out it was her late husband who was channeling me so I said, I think your late husband channeled me this morning. I wasn't even worried that she would think I was crazy. I told her all that happened and she started crying! She told me about her husband for the first time. She told me that he courted her by bringing her red roses and left them strategically so she would know they were from him. She said had he been alive today, she would have received 30 red roses! I had this tingling feeling and I was so happy I had this experience. Then she told me that there was a tree at their house where flocks of birds would come and her husband and she loved to watch them together. **OMG! I couldn't believe it but I experienced it wide awake! This was my first-time channeling someone I did NOT know!** She also said he was always so anxious to give her the flowers and would get very child-like excited to see her reaction! OK, then **I** started crying. What is more incredible than that experience is that our friendship has grown greatly. We have worked on several church events that have brought in donations

FAR above any other events -to- date at the church. **I told her that I feel we are destined to do great things together.** She looked a little scared. **Well since then, she was elected the Chair and I the Vice-Chair for the Church Guild and I had a feeling God had big plans for us to grow this Ministry to promote fellowship and to help the less fortunate families in the parish.**

Year 2016

I was very excited to help lead the Church Guild this year. **I felt a strong desire to re-build a group of creative people who could craft items for a yearly Holiday Boutique and Bake Sale.** I wrote a proposal and named the group, Creative Circle, because we would get together around a table and create handcrafted items for the Boutique. Our priest gave us his blessing to meet at the church and agreed we could have a Holiday Boutique and Bake Sale. I donated my supplies I had accumulated over the years when I used to have an annual Holiday Boutique in my house and taught the volunteers several craft techniques and let them show their talent and creativity and most of all to have fun. Well, we started in June with about 10 volunteers from the parish and by the October we had close to 40 volunteers and hundreds of beautiful handcrafted items. We scheduled the Boutique and Bake Sale for a 3day weekend in November. The Creative Circle volunteers and many others from the parish organized, set up, greeted customers and closed the event successfully resulting in an unbelievable positive outcome for the church and fun for all who experienced and volunteered at the event.

In September, my dad, now 93 years old, was diagnosed with COPD and had to be on oxygen. He was very unhappy about this constraint or disability in his life. He just always worked so hard to be healthy and vibrant. I was very concerned about his disposition, trying to help him cope. One night I was going to sleep and my grandmother (my dad's mother) came to me in a vision. I said out loud, "Hi Grandma." She smiled at me and then she was gone. I thought maybe she came to thank me for taking care of my dad.

Shortly thereafter, early in October, my dad became very ill. He was in and out of the hospital a few times and found out he had a very serious infection. My brother and I were by his side and very worried, but the hospital kept encouraging us that he would improve. We took turns staying with our dad. I had afternoon duty one day and my dad was sleeping. He was on a respirator also. So I just stood by his bed and held his hand. They told me he was weak and could not sit up. I told him I was there and he would be ok. He then squeezed my hand so hard that it hurt. I waited for him to release a little and told him I would be back tomorrow. I went home and went to sleep. Very early the next morning my phone rang and the hospital told me to come now and that he was crashing. My brother and I raced to the hospital and held his hand, telling him we loved him and I leaned over close to his ear and told him I loved him and he could go to the light now. He then passed peacefully. My rock was gone. I guess my grandmother was trying to tell me more and that she was happily waiting for him in heaven. The next few days were a blur as we prepared for his service and burial. I had been fighting with the cemetery about my dad's burial plot that was stolen and even though they told me it was fixed, they never sent me paperwork. I was so worried that he would not be buried where he wished to be buried. I awoke the next morning and something told me to call my dear friend who gave me that short term job earlier. She lives near the cemetery so I called to ask her to help as I live in Southern California and the cemetery is in Northern California. My friend cleared her work calendar that day for me and spoke to the cemetery resulting in a call to me that all was fine. I was so relieved and will be forever grateful to her. The son of the mortuary owner who spoke to my dad earlier as family, now would help my dad be laid to rest. He came to the cemetery with us and when the Military Guard handed me the folded flag that draped my dad's coffin, everyone was crying. All of a sudden, the son of the mortuary owner started talking and recalling his conversation with my dad months earlier out loud and said something that made us all laugh. Afterwards he said to my brother and me that he had no control and just started talking out-loud. He said he never did that before and did not understand why he spoke. My brother and I knew it was our dad telling us not to be sad.

The next day was my niece's wedding and even though I was struggling with my grieving, I attended her wedding for me AND my dad. My dad so wanted to go to her wedding and to walk her down the aisle as my niece's dad would not be at the wedding. The wedding was in an outside garden. As we are all looking to the entrance where the bride walks in, I saw a VERY bright light in the form of a person standing right inside the entrance where my niece walked in. At first, I thought it was the sun but then I realized it was my dad. He so wanted to go to her wedding. I was so happy he was there. I went home the next day and that night the house was quiet, just me and my dog, Katie. I always left one light on for Katie as she was nearly blind. I went to bed. In the middle of the night I went to check on Katie and a light that I never use was turned on. I think my dad wanted me to know he was watching over me. The next day, my best friend and soul sister since 7th grade called me. She said my dad came to her in her dreams. He said he wanted her to tell me that he was fine and that I could get on with my life now. He also told her that "her" dad who died a few months earlier, had been one of the first to greet him in heaven. My dad told her he feels better than he had for a long time.

Year 2017

Katie and I were both grieving the loss of my dad. I would find Katie in my dad's bedroom lying next to the desk he sat at and sometimes I saw her looking up as if she saw him standing next to her. Then Katie started having seizures and she was getting weaker. I knew her time was coming or maybe my dad was calling to her. I had her for 15 ½ years, getting her when she was about 8 weeks old. As was my first Cocker, Molly, Katie was my baby, too. I lost her on Jan. 26, on my dad's birthday. It was barely past midnight when her heart stopped in the emergency room. How could I cope with grieving for her AND my dad? I tried to sleep off and on and so wanted to know she was ok in heaven. I was sitting up on the sofa and I dozed off in the afternoon that day. As I began to awaken from my nap, there Katie was in a vision, she was laying on her back in some grassy area with her head tilted back looking at me and her tongue hanging out of the side of her mouth. She had been running hard and was enjoying a rest in the grass. She looked at me and I knew she was happy and healthy again because when she was young, she always loved to run and be active and her eyes told me she was ok. I felt she was happy to see me, too. I told her I loved her and then she was gone. I tell people she must have run all the way to heaven and I am sure my mom and dad were there to greet her! Once again God answered my prayer.

In the last month or so while I am still grieving and my house is so quiet, I wonder what now? Last month I co-led a Fashion Show fundraiser for my church which was a huge success with doubling attendance from last year! Once again, I feel God continues to guide me. I sense my life is changing in a big way. I am now finished with caring for my parents. Usually when I lose one of my dogs, I go right out and get another, but this time my feelings are different. While I miss Katie so much, I feel like I am waiting for something or someone. In the meantime, I am motivated to clean out closets and donate the items to charity, to begin another year of the Creative Circle with my church, to visit some friends and I have a desire to travel this year, but I am unsure of my destination. God will guide me in divine time.

A few months back, I was sleeping one night and early in the morning when the sun was rising, I heard a dog crying like it was hurting or very unhappy. I am slowly awakening and thinking this is so unusual because in our community, people who have pets do NOT leave their dogs outside because we have occasional coyotes in our yards. As I am awakening, I am worried about this dog so I thought I should get up and check on this. As I opened my eyes, right beside my bed on the floor was my deceased dog, Katie sitting there looking up at me, very happy to visit and see me. I smiled, too and said hi. She then left and I no longer heard any dog noises. Isn't it ironic that both she and my earlier Cocker, Molly, both came to see me after their death?

Well I guess you will not be surprised when I tell you that I was nominated to be Chairperson for my church Guild and my new friend is Vice Chairperson. Yes, this new friend is another soulmate of mine and we have discovered so MANY parts of our lives in common, too many to mention. We finished 2017 with our Annual Holiday Craft Boutique and Bake Sale, yet with greater success than last year! We have encouraged growth of the Guild membership as well as expanding help to needy families in the community.

Year 2018

So, what is next for me? Well I can only tell you that I feel like God is telling me to wait for someone or something again. I am feeling children are involved. I feel I may be traveling or moving. I think this is why I have not adopted another doggie yet. I did happen to run into my veterinarian recently and he told me to go get another Cocker and he told me I am a very good Mom. I am also feeling like I should free up my time from the church Guild so I am available. I feel the need to purge unneeded items in my home so I will do some Spring cleaning. I so miss my parents and my dog, Katie. Recently, in the middle of the night, I was quickly awakened when Katie came to visit and she kissed me on my mouth. Christmas is particularly hard for me as it is my favorite time of year and I want to regain the joy and excitement again of Christ's Birthday and a Giving Season.

Year 2019

I continue to lead the Church Guild and work with a team to generate or sponsor various events and activities. I have been giving emotional support to my oldest brother. One particular day I was thinking of him and his wife and all of a sudden, I started crying very hard and then my deceased mom told me to write this message down and give it to my brother.

"Honey, this is Mom. I love you Tony. I want you to know that I am with you and Kathi today. I have always been proud of my first born. I will watch over you and Kathi. Everything will be ok Tony. She knows that you love her and always will. You are a good man and Dad and I are very proud of you and how you help all of your brothers and sisters. When you feel you need us Tony, talk or pray to us. We hear you and are with you honey. All our love, Mom and Dad."

I could hardly type fast enough as I was crying so hard and I never learned how to type. When I gave it later to my brother, he also cried and then we both cried again. He keeps this message with him at all times now and reads it whenever he needs strength and comfort as he continues to deal with his hardship.

I feel God is encouraging me to finish this book and to share it with others so they can focus on the good parts of their lives, learn from their mistakes and to listen to their inner guidance that will bring them happiness and fulfillment in life in spite of the all the turmoil and strife in the world today. Making the world a better place begins with each of us believing, committing and contributing in positive thinking, in giving and sharing, and in our faith to live our life purpose.